Amazing Nature

Night Movers

D1402289

Matt Turner

Heinemann Library
Chicago, Illinois

Customer Service 888-454-2279
Visit our website at www.heinemannlibrary.com

Produced for Heinemann Library by Discovery Books Limited
Originated by Ambassador Litho Ltd
Printed in China by South China Printing Company

08 07 06 05 04
10 9 8 7 6 5 4 3 2 1

Library of Congress Cataloging-in-Publication Data
Turner, Matt, 1964-
  Night movers / Matt Turner.
      p. cm. -- (Amazing nature)
Summary: Describes the after-dark activities of many nocturnal animals.
Includes bibliographical references (p.   ) and index.
  ISBN 1-4034-4706-3 (Hardcover) -- ISBN 1-4034-5402-7 (pbk.)
  1. Nocturnal animals--Juvenile literature. [1. Nocturnal animals.] I.
Title. II. Series.
  QL755.5.T88 2003
  591.5'18--dc22

                          2003022042

Acknowledgments
The publisher would like to thank the following for permission to reproduce photographs:
p. 4 Robert Erwin/Natural History Photographic Agency; p. 5 John Hawkins/FLPA; p. 6 Adrian Hepworth/Natural History Photographic Agency; p. 7 John Mitchell/Oxford Scientific Films; p. 8 L. West/FLPA; p. 9 Photodisc; p. 10 Jane Burton/Bruce Coleman Collection; p. 11 Paulo De Oliveira/Oxford Scientific Films; p. 12 David M. Dennis/Oxford Scientific Films; p. 13 F. Lanting/Minden Pictures/FLPA; p. 14 Corbis; p. 15 Tui de Roy/Minden Pictures/FLPA; p. 16 Gerard Lacz/FLPA; p. 17 Daniel Heuclin/Natural History Photographic Agency; p. 18 Alain Compost/Bruce Coleman Collection; p. 19 Terry Whittaker/FLPA; p. 20 Bert & Babs Wells/Oxford Scientific Films; p. 21 Kim Taylor/Bruce Coleman Collection; p. 22 Joe Blossom/Natural History Photographic Agency; p. 23 David Hosking/FLPA; p. 24 Geoff Moon/FLPA; p. 25A Bill Coster/Natural History Photographic Agency; p. 25B Howard Hall/Oxford Scientific Films; p. 26 Kim Taylor/Bruce Coleman Collection; p. 27 Satoshi Kuribayashi/Oxford Scientific Films; p. 28 Kim Taylor/Bruce Coleman Collection; p. 29 David M. Dennis/Oxford Scientific Films.

Cover photograph of a barn owl: Manfred Danegger/Natural History Photographic Agency.

Every effort has been made to contact copyright holders of any material reproduced in this book. Any omissions will be rectified in subsequent printings if notice is given to the publisher.

Some words are shown in bold, **like this.** You can find out what they mean by looking in the glossary.

Contents

Living in the Dark 4

Safe from the Sun 6

Saving Your Skin 8

Secrets of the Sand 10

Not So Blind! 12

It's a Hoot 14

Night Hunters 16

Leaping and Creeping 18

On Soft Wings 20

Cloaked in Secrecy 22

Night Flight .24

Night-Lights .26

Fact File 28

Glossary . . . . *.30*

More Books to Read . . . . *.31*

Index . . . . *.32*

Living in the Dark

We humans are creatures of the day. For most of us, there is little for us to do at night except sleep. After all, our eyes cannot see in the dark, and our bodies need to rest. But for many animals, night is the best time to be active. We call these animals **nocturnal**.

There are many reasons for being nocturnal. Some animals are in danger of drying out during the day. They are more comfortable in the cooler night air. A lot of small **mammals** feel safer in the darkness, when many hunting animals are asleep. Or perhaps the animals are hunters, with super **senses** that can find **prey** as easily as if it were broad daylight.

The large ears of a desert fox hear as much sound as possible in the dark of night, helping it find its prey.

Huge eyes and pin-sharp hearing allow an owl to strike accurately. The bird makes no noise as it swoops down, so the mouse is caught by surprise.

Some animals prefer to be active during the **twilight** hours around sunrise and sunset. There is a little light to see by at those times, but it is still dark enough for them to hide from hunters. These are known as crepuscular animals.

Many night animals have special skills. Some small mammals have developed enormous eyes to see better in the dark. Bats use sounds to find their way. Birds use the stars to find their way through the night sky. Many plants are active at night too, attracting moths and bats with strong perfume or sweet **nectar**. In fact, the more you find out about nightlife, the more it seems that we humans are sleeping through some of nature's greatest marvels!

Safe from the Sun

Many small creatures hide under stones and logs during the day. If they did not, the sun would dry them out and kill them. These animals include slugs and snails, which belong to a larger group of animals known as **mollusks.** Millions of years ago, all mollusks lived in the sea. Even after this long period of time, slugs and snails are not completely **adapted** to living out of the water, so they must stay damp. They usually only come out at night when the air is cooler and less likely to dry them out. Slugs and snails spend the night eating plants and soil.

Although they have tiny eyes, slugs and snails can move around in the darkness and find food just by touching, tasting, and smelling with their long feelers.

Dark and damp

Wood lice, centipedes, and millipedes look as though they wear suits of armor. The armor is actually an outer **skeleton**. It is tough, but it does not prevent moisture from escaping from the animals' bodies. These animals have to spend the daytime in damp places to avoid drying out. They run away from bright lights and find hiding places under stones or fallen leaves.

Wood lice feed on rotting plants, but centipedes eat other animals. At night the centipede slips out to hunt, running quickly on its many legs. The long **antennae** on its head help it find its way by tasting the air and touching the ground.

Although it is related to the centipede, the millipede is a plant-eater, not a hunter. At night the millipede pushes slowly through fallen leaves, tapping them with its antennae to find its way.

*Centipedes have fangs full of **venom** for killing the animals they hunt. Giant centipedes like this one can capture and eat frogs, toads, and baby birds.*

Saving Your Skin

For many frogs and toads, night is the safest time to be active. Frogs and toads are **amphibians,** animals that live both in water and on land. Amphibians have unusual, soft skin. As long as their skin stays wet, they can drink and breathe through it. After heavy rains, they may be seen out and about during the day.

In dry weather, frogs and toads avoid the sun. They stay wet by resting in damp places such as in long grass or under logs or stones. The American toad digs itself a small daytime bed among fallen leaves. It stays cool and hides from hungry hunters, such as raccoons and skunks. At night it comes out to hunt **insects,** slugs, and worms.

American toads travel at night to pools of water to look for **mates.** Getting there is dangerous, for they often have to cross busy roads. The males call loudly, night after night, to attract females.

Having red eyes helps the red-eyed tree frog stay alive. When a bird swoops down on the frog to eat it, the frog opens its eyes. The sudden flash of red frightens the bird away.

Life on a leaf

Many frogs live in trees. The red-eyed tree frog lives in warm, rainy, **tropical** forests from Mexico to Colombia. It spends the day resting in the branches, usually lying upside down against the cool underside of a leaf. **Suction cups** on its toes keep it from falling off. Birds like to eat frogs, but they cannot see a tree frog hidden under a leaf.

On some nights, the female frog climbs down to a pool of water. She soaks up water through her skin, just like a sponge. Then she climbs up to a branch that hangs over the pool. She lays a few eggs on a leaf. On each egg is a layer of jelly, made sticky by the water from her body. The jelly keeps the eggs healthy. Tadpoles hatch from the eggs about five days later and drop straight into the pool of water below.

Secrets of the Sand

Few animals live in deserts, which are often hot during the day and are always very dry. Animals that are able to survive in the desert hide during the heat of the day and come out at night. They include **rodents** like gerbils, pocket mice, and kangaroo rats. Rodents are **mammals** with special front teeth used for nibbling. During the day, these desert rodents plug the entrances to their underground burrows with sand. This keeps the air inside cool and damp, and shuts out snakes. After sunset, the desert air grows cool and the rodents dig their way out. They move quietly in the darkness, using their long whiskers and good sense of smell to find plant seeds to eat. The rodents must listen for foxes and wildcats. The foxes and wildcats listen carefully, too, ready to pounce if they hear a rodent moving nearby.

In the hot sun of north Africa's large deserts, a gerbil would only survive for about two hours before dying of water loss. So it hides in a burrow by day, coming out at night to feed.

Hidden danger

The scorpion is a small but dangerous desert animal. It has eight legs, like a spider, and a pair of claws used for holding food and digging burrows. Tough, waxy armor covers its long, flat body. Although it has weak eyes, the scorpion can see well enough to find its way around by starlight and moonlight.

The scorpion hides in a hole or under a stone, only coming out at sunset.

The scorpion hunts almost everything that moves, including **insects** and lizards. How does it find them? Tiny hairs all over the scorpion's body and legs feel **vibrations**. They can sense creatures moving a long way away. A deadly stinger in the scorpion's tail poisons its **prey.** However, there is often little to eat in the desert, so the scorpion may go hungry for weeks.

Not So Blind!

When the sun sets, most birds go to sleep and bats take over the skies. Like a lot of birds that fly during the day, many bats eat **insects**. Unlike most birds, however, the bats can find their way in the dark. By feeding at night, bats avoid competing with the birds for food.

Most **species** of bat can "see" using a technique called echolocation (eck-oh-loh-kay-shun). To do this, a bat squeaks then listens to the echoes of the squeak. The echo bouncing back from each object tells the bat where that object is. Listening to its echoes, a bat can fly around trees and buildings in total darkness. It can even follow and catch a flying insect.

*This greater horseshoe bat is using sound to follow its moth **prey**. It squeaks through its nose, which has a special shape that sends the sounds in the right direction. The squeaks are too high-pitched for humans to hear.*

Like insect-eating bats, the bulldog bat listens to the echoes from its voice to "see." It listens for ripples in water made by fish. Then the bat lowers its back claws into the water and scoops out a meal.

Midnight feast

Not all bats eat insects. Fruit bats eat ripe fruit. They feed at night so they do not have to compete with animals that eat fruit during the day, such as birds and monkeys. Most fruit bats use their eyes, not their voices, to see in the dark. They also use their keen noses to sniff their way to the fruit. Other plant parts are good to eat, too. Pallas's long-tongued bat licks the **nectar** from passion flowers, which only bloom at night.

The American bulldog bat is one of a small number of fishing bats. It flies low over water and can catch fish in total darkness. The vampire bat drinks blood. Landing on the ground near a sleeping animal, it creeps closer. Without waking the animal, the bat bites a small wound and laps up the blood that flows out.

It's a Hoot

Most owls hunt at night. By doing this they avoid feeding at the same time as the birds that hunt by day. Owls catch small creatures like mice, voles, and young rabbits.

An owl's eyeballs are very large. They gather so much light that they are about two-and-a-half times better than human eyes at seeing in the dark. The eyeballs fit the head so snugly that they can barely move to look left or right. Instead, the owl turns its whole head. The owl's ears are so keen, they can hear the faint rustle of a mouse creeping through leaves. Its feathers have fluffy edges that muffle sound as the owl flies. The attack is so quiet that its **prey** has no chance of running away.

The great horned owl is one of North America's largest owls. It hunts animals up to the size of hares. The horns are really tufts of feathers.

Beaks with a difference

Nightjars are birds that hunt **insects** at night. They swoop down after moths or beetles. They are most successful at sunset on warm evenings when there is still a little light they can use to see. A nightjar's beak is surrounded by bristles, which spread like a net to help it trap prey. During the day, nightjars rest very still on branches. With their patterned brown feathers, they look just like pieces of branches and are very hard to see. This protects them from larger animals looking for food during the day.

One of the strangest night birds is the brown kiwi of New Zealand. Like many birds of New Zealand, it cannot fly. Instead, it walks. The kiwi's nostrils are near the tip of its long beak, and it has a wonderful sense of smell. The bird scratches at the ground with strong claws and pushes its beak into the earth to sniff out worms, its favorite food.

Long, stiff whiskers surround the kiwi's beak. They help the bird feel the ground and find food in the darkness.

Night Hunters

Many **mammals** that hunt at night have superb eyesight, thanks to an extra-shiny surface inside each eye that catches the light. At **twilight,** cats can see six times better than humans can. Jaguars and leopards are big cats that hunt at night. They creep up slowly on deer, pigs, and other **prey** that feed at night, then pounce on them suddenly. Their patterned coats break up their outlines, making these big cats almost invisible in the moonlight.

A jaguar has long, stiff hairs, called whiskers, around its eyes and nose. The whiskers brush against rocks, plants, and other objects. They allow the jaguar to feel its way around in total darkness. At night, the pupils—the dark centers—in a jaguar's eyes open wide to let in as much light as possible. By day, the pupils narrow to slits to stop strong light from harming the eyes.

The raccoon is a night hunter that eats almost anything. It is especially fond of crayfish. Crayfish are small creatures like lobsters that live in streams. The raccoon uses its paws as we would use our hands. It turns over stones and feels in the water for the crayfish.

You can see the pits in the head of this pit viper, just behind the nostrils. The pits can sense anything that is hotter than they are.

Heat seekers

Pit vipers are snakes with a secret weapon for hunting at night. Their name comes from two pits, or dents, found in their heads. These pits help the viper feel heat. A pit viper eats mice, rabbits, birds, and other small animals. First, it finds an animal with its eyes or nose. Then it sneaks up to within 2 feet (60 centimeters) of the animal. At this distance, the pits in the viper's head can feel the heat of the animal's body. Just as our ears can hear whether a noise comes from the left or right, the snake's pits can feel where the heat is coming from. Very quickly, the snake strikes at the hottest area. It injects a dose of **venom** that will eventually kill its prey. Having pits that can sense heat means that the snake can track its dying prey in the darkness.

Leaping and Creeping

On a warm night on an island in Southeast Asia, a tiny **mammal** clings to a branch with long, bony fingers. It has shell-like ears and huge, round eyes that stare into the gloom. Twisting its head around to look fully over its back, the animal suddenly leaps into the air and lands on the next branch. This is a tarsier out on the hunt. A tarsier eats all kinds of animals, from ants and beetles to lizards, birds, and snakes. Its enormous ears and eyes help it find **prey** in the dark. Once it has found a victim, the tarsier leaps and pins it down with its hands.

Each of the western tarsier's eyes weighs more than its brain! Its eyes are so big that they cannot move much in its head. Instead, the tarsier turns its head to look around, like an owl.

The slow loris moves very slowly. This one has successfully crept up on an insect. Like humans, a slow loris has a thumb-and-finger grip that helps it grab food or hold tightly to branches.

Quick and slow

Tarsiers belong to an animal group called the **prosimians**. Prosimians are very distantly related to monkeys and apes, and they all have large eyes. Most prosimians have superb eyesight and hearing. With these senses they can hunt at night and enjoy food that many other animals cannot find.

Other prosimians include bush babies, lorises, and pottos. A bush baby leaps among the branches like an acrobat, trusting its eyes to correctly judge each jump. It is so quick with its hands that it can snatch flies and moths from the air. Lorises and pottos move so slowly that they can sneak up on moths without being seen. If a loris is disturbed by a strange noise, it stands completely still, sometimes for hours on end. When it feels safe again, the loris continues its snail-like creep.

On Soft Wings

Moths and butterflies drink **nectar** from flowers. Because most moths feed at night and most butterflies by day, they stay out of each other's way. Moths also fly at night to avoid birds.

When a moth dips its tongue into a flower, the flower's dusty **pollen** brushes off on the moth's head. The moth moves that pollen from one plant to another. The pollen helps the plant make seeds that later grow into new plants. This is called **pollination**. Some plants make extra nectar at night, because this is when moths visit. The flowers give off scents to attract the moths. Often the flowers are white or cream, colors that show up well in the darkness. The plants and moths need each other: the moths need food, the plants need pollination.

This hawkmoth flies at night. It is named for its powerful, hovering flight, which is like that of a hawk. Flight is tiring, so the moth feeds on sugary nectar to keep up its energy.

Perfume in the air

Flower scents often seem stronger at night, especially in summer. This is because cool night air moves less than warm daytime air, so the scents do not blow away. Instead, they slowly drift. Scents help moths find the flowers.

A different sort of scent also helps a moth find a partner. The female moth gives off a special scent called a **pheromone**(fair-uh-moan). The male moth can smell her pheromone from far away. To him, the pheromone is like the world's most delicious perfume. He follows the trail, and eventually finds the female. Then they can **mate**.

The male emperor moth smells the air with his very feathery antennae. On a still night, he can detect a female moth's scent from miles away.

Cloaked in Secrecy

Mice, rats, rabbits, and deer are just a few of the many **mammals** that hide by day to escape **predators**. They come out at night to feed. Some night mammals have big, bulging eyes that see well in the dark, but almost all have a keen sense of smell.

The muntjac (mun-jack) has both. It is a tiny deer that lives in forests in parts of Asia and feeds on plants at night. Tigers, jackals, and big snakes all like to eat muntjacs, so the deer walks very carefully through the forest, trying not to make a sound. If it hears a strange noise, it first stands still and listens. Then it barks loudly to warn other muntjacs of the danger.

The muntjac stays out of danger by being alert at all times. A spotted coat helps to break up the fawn's outline during its first few months. The spots then fade.

Danger in the dark

The brushtail possum lives in the holes of trees in Australia. It rubs its strong body smell on its home tree to tell other possums to stay away. At night the brushtail possum climbs along branches and nibbles leaves, fruit, and flowers. But even though it eats at night, it is not safe from all hunters.

The brushtail possum is an excellent climber. Its sharp claws give it a good grip on bark, and the end of its tail can be used like another arm, curling around branches to hold on tight.

The scrub python is Australia's largest snake. It can grow to be over twenty feet (six meters) long. The lace goanna is a lizard that can climb trees. It is as large as a human. Both the snake and the goanna find **prey** by flicking out their tongues to taste scents in the air. The scrub python can swallow a possum whole!

Night Flight

As the seasons change throughout the year, many birds move from one part of the world to another. This is called **migration**. Birds may migrate to find a better supply of food or to **rear** their chicks. Many of them migrate at night. This is true of small songbirds, which get tired quickly. Flying is easier at night because the air is cooler and calmer. Also, they are less likely to be attacked by hawks at night because hawks fly during the daytime. Migrating birds travel in flocks. They call to each other once in awhile with very short bursts of song. This helps them to stay in touch with each other and avoid getting lost.

At night during April and May, the tiny Tasmanian silvereye migrates 992 miles (1,600 km) from the island of Tasmania to as far north as Queensland in Australia.

Which way home?

How do migrating birds find their way? By day, they use the sun's position as well as objects on the ground like hills and rivers. By night, birds follow the stars. As chicks in the nest, they will have stared up at the sky and learned the star patterns.

Amazingly, birds may also have a natural **compass.** Our planet is like a giant magnet, which is why a compass always points north and south. Inside a bird's head are tiny grains of a magnetic material called **magnetite.** The bird produces magnetite naturally. Scientists believe the magnetite tells the bird which way is north.

On a clear, moonlit night you may see birds flying on migration. Ducks and geese make a V-shaped group. Small songbirds fly in a loose flock.

magnetism links

Many other animals, including fish, whales, spiny lobsters, bees, butterflies, and perhaps turtles, too, are thought to use magnetism to find their way, although they usually use other **senses** as well.

Spiny lobsters migrate in the Atlantic Ocean. Playing follow-the-leader is a good way of getting where they want to go, but it probably also helps that they feel the earth's magnetic pull.

Night-Lights

Have you tried signaling to a friend by flashing a flashlight? This is what a glowworm does. A glowworm is not actually a worm at all, but a beetle. Its "torch" is inside the tip of its abdomen, the back part of the body. The beetle's body mixes chemicals with oxygen to make light. The light is not hot, like a real flashlight, but cold, so it does not hurt the glowworm. At night, the female glowworm climbs up a grass stem and turns on her light like a little lighthouse. If she is lucky, a male will see her light and come to **mate** with her.

This female glowworm is trying to attract a male. She does not have the hard, shiny wing covers that we see on most kinds of beetles, and that is why she is said to look like a worm.

These male Japanese fireflies have gathered to attract females. All the males flash their lights at once. Any females nearby will recognize these lights and flash back. Their replies are a way of saying, "I see you. Now you can see me. Come here and we'll mate."

Flashy behavior

Many of these glowing beetles do not simply glow. They actually flash their lights on and off. Beetles that do this are called fireflies or lightning bugs. In North America, a male firefly flies near the ground in fields and briefly flashes his light. Any female that sees him flashes an answer. He then answers back, and eventually they meet up and mate. There may be many different **species** of fireflies living in one field. However, each species recognizes the right partner by a special code of flashes. Some fireflies turn this into a deadly trick. By flashing a different code, a female may pretend to be a different species. When the male of that species arrives, she eats him!

Fact File

At night, tiny animals in the sea—such as young fish and crabs—swim to the surface to feed on small plants. They do not swim up by day, as they may be seen and eaten by large fish. However, they are not completely safe at night. Herring, squid, and lantern fish all swim up at night to feed on the mass of tiny animals.

A tawny owl does not actually sing "tu-whit tu-whoo." This is the sound of two owls having a conversation! One owl says "tu-whit," and its mate answers "tu-whoo." Hooting helps the birds stay in touch in the darkness.

Glowworms glow at all stages of life. Even the eggs have a faint glow, and young glowworms give off a bright light. This may be to warn other animals that they are in fact poisonous.

The red fox hunts in the middle of the night, listening for the sounds of moving animals. It has such good hearing that it can pick up the faint sound of a worm scraping against fallen leaves as it wiggles out of the ground 3.3 feet (1 meter) away.

The tough outer **skeleton** of a scorpion contains a thin layer of a material called hyaline. At night, scientists look for scorpions by shining a special purple light called ultraviolet light, which makes the hyaline glow in the dark. Scientists have also discovered **fossil** scorpions up to 300 million years old. They still glow!

Like glowworms, the Bermuda fireworm makes light in order to meet a mate. It lives in the sea, and normally stays on the sea bed. On certain nights in summer, about an hour after sunset, the female rises near the water's surface. There, she swims in circles and glows green. The male worm sees her glow and swims toward it. When the two animals meet, they **mate.**

In North America, the great horned owl and the red-tailed hawk both hunt hares—the owl by night, the hawk by day. This allows owls and hawks to live in the same area and not compete with one another. On the Galápagos Islands in the Pacific Ocean, the short-eared owl likes to hunt both day and night. But one of the owl's neighbors is the Galápagos hawk. Therefore, the owl can only fly at night. If it appears by day, the hawk attacks it.

Glossary

adapt   to change in a way that better suits an animal to its surroundings

amphibian   animal that may live on land but must spend part of its life in the water

antenna (more than one are called antennae)   feelers that stick out from an insect's head. They are used to smell and touch.

compass   instrument that uses a magnet to find north, south, east, and west

fossil   hard, preserved remains of a plant or an animal

insect   animal with six legs and three body parts: head, thorax, and abdomen

magnetite   form of iron that is found naturally in the bodies of many animals and acts like a compass

mammal   warm-blooded, furry animal that feeds its young on milk produced by the mother

mate   to mix male and female cells to create young

migration   movement of animals from one area to another as the seasons or living conditions change

mollusk   member of a group of soft-bodied animals. Snails, slugs, squids, and octopuses are all mollusks.

nectar   sugary liquid produced by flowers

nocturnal   being active at night

pheromone   chemical that an animal produces to make another animal do something

pollen   dust-like grains from the male part of a flower

pollination   when the male part of a plant fertilizes the female part of another plant

predator   animal that hunts other living animals

prey   animal that is eaten by another animal

prosimian   mammal related to monkeys and apes

rear   to look after young animals until they are grown

rodent   mammal with constantly growing front teeth that gnaw hard food

sense   special power such as smell, touch, sight, or hearing that helps animals know their surroundings

skeleton   framework that supports and protects a body

species   type of living thing

suction cup   soft, saucer-shaped pad that grips surfaces by forcing air out of the cup

tropical   hot regions of the world where the sun is directly overhead for part of the year

twilight   near-dark period of sunrise or sunset

venom   poison that one animal injects into another

vibration   slight movement of the air or ground

More Books to Read

Craig, Janet. *Amazing World of Night Creatures.* Mahwah, N.J.: Troll Communications, 1997.

Fitzsimons, Cecilia. *Wolves Howl at the Moon: And Other Amazing Facts about Creatures of the Night.* Brookfield, Conn.: Millbrook Press, 2000.

Fredericks, Anthony D. and Sneed B. Collard. *Amazing Animals: Nature's Most Incredible Creatures.* Chanhassen, Minn.: Creative Publishing International, 2000.

Index

bats 5, 12–13
Bermuda fireworms 29
brushtail possums 23
bush babies 19

centipedes 7
crabs 28
crayfish 17

deer 16, 22
desert foxes 4, 10
deserts 10–11

echolocation 12
eyes 14, 16, 18

fireflies 27
fish 28
fossils 29
frogs 8–9

gerbils 10
glowworms 26, 28

hawks 24, 29
hyaline 29

jaguars 16

kiwis 15

lace goanna lizards 23
leopards 16
lorises 19

magnetite 25

mice 10, 22
migration 24–25
millipedes 7
mollusks 6
moths 15, 20–21
muntjacs 22

nightjars 15

owls 5, 14, 28, 29

pheromones 21
pit vipers 17
pollination 20
pottos 19
prosimians 18–19

rabbits 22
raccoons 8, 17
rats 10, 22
red foxes 28
rodents 10

scorpions 11, 29
scrub pythons 23
skunks 8
slugs 6
snails 6
spiny lobsters 25
squids 28

tarsiers 18
Tasmanian silvereyes 24
toads 8

wood lice 7